I Open Myself to You, Oh Lord!

Reflections of my Spiritual Journey

By Beverly Ann Wernet

Cover photos are of Onondaga Lake, Liverpool, New York.

All photos were produced by the author. On the shores of Onondaga Lake, "where God rested His Hand after creation," Hiawatha brought together the warrior tribes of: Seneca, Cayuga, Onondaga,

Oneida, and Mohawk. Here was signed the peace treaty which created the Iroquois Confederacy. This historic peace treaty remains in existence yet today. May the viewers of my photos experience this peacefulness.

www.xulonpress.com

I Open Myself to You, Oh Lord!

Reflections of my Spiritual Journey

Table of Contents

Acknowledgements

I wish to thank those who have supported me during the "crosses" of my life and the formative years of my spirituality: my brother Art and his wife Pat (don't forget our Bailey's day!), my sister Beth (shop ... listen ... go shop!), and my friends Lois and Vince ("mom and dad") and Marybeth (who wants to knock at this next door?).

Thanks to you, Father Tom, who planted the "seed" in my heart to write and still guides me on my spiritual path with the Lord. You led me to the door and helped me open it, to enjoy the windswept journey of experiencing the Lord! Through you, I have learned and experienced God's Peace, Calm and Love ... may you too!

Thank you Doug, my husband, for sharing your love, stability, honesty, and friendship with me, and for opening yourself up to God and accepting His Blessings upon us. We are so blessed and thankful to the Lord.

Thanks to Jane, my mother-in-law, for her encouragement and inspiration to get through whatever life "deals" me.

To Amos and Annie, our two little bright-eyed and warm buddies, who greet us endlessly with wagging tails and cold noses to prod us on as a gift from God reflecting His Love. I thank Him for you.

Thank you, mom and dad, for placing the spiritual building blocks in me. And now my home is complete with the door open to the Lord and the windows to share the view of those stars of the Lord that I saw in your dying eyes.

Most importantly ... Thank You, Lord ... In the name of God my Father, for waiting so patiently for my return and lovingly welcoming me back, and of Jesus His Son, for giving Your Heart to me and accepting me as Your bride, and of the Holy Spirit, for dwelling within me and "gifting" me with these writings to reach to you, the readers. Amen.

And ... thank you readers, for allowing God's inspiration to guide you to my writings. In opening yourself to the Lord, may you experience His Love and Peace, and the many gifts He offers you.

"Amos and Annie"

Forward

Bev Wernet in this, her first published work, has woven a richly textured pattern that will deeply touch and illumine the soul along its spiritual path to God. In the long and illustrious tradition of a Catherine of Siena or a Teresa of Carmel, the author is sensitively attuned to the delicate undulations of the Spirit of Jesus expressed with such fine and poetic imagery. Her carefully chosen words stir the soul and fire the imagination. You will discover in this little gem of a book a gold mine of interwoven threads of thought, reflection, prayer and meditation that give expression to what we often find so difficult to put into words.

May you also, as I did, discover in this profound unveiling of one woman's soul a revelation of your own quest for spiritual Grail — a quest that begins and ends with the journey deep within. What this spiritual mother tenders us is indeed only a tantalizing aperitif to a much richer fare. I believe that her work will have achieved its end if for no other reason than because it will have led the soul on a search more deeply within for what Jesus promised another woman – the woman of Samaria at Jacob's Well: *"a fountain within him leaping up to provide eternal life."* (John 4:14).

It has been my joy and my delight to have accompanied the author and joined in her spiritual quest for *"the foundation within!"*

Father Cebula

Open the Drawers
of Memories

Events occur in life. You experience them, enjoy them, and hate them. Just like clothes, you put them away in drawers with the intent to reconsider at a later time. Then days and years pass. You open the drawers, sort through the events, and choose to throw them out or keep them to "fit" in your life as remembrances. You reflect, maybe it will "fit" right this time or maybe later, or this one just makes you feel happy or this one sad. Some have deep purpose and meaning. Some you just want to forget. Some you pull out and will wear and wear and wear. Memories: a death ... a death ... a priest ... and a weaver.

Through my writings, I wish to share with you this journey of discovery and wonderment which has provided fulfillment and meaning to the unexplainable and resulted in my loving, spiritual relationship with the Lord.

As you read my writings, please allow yourself to experience God's Tenderness and Love, as I have

with Him. The undulation of the depths of my medi-
tations has profoundly affected the type of verse
that I wrote at the time of each experience. At times,
this led me to experience the human limitation of
expressing the wonderment of the Lord. So please
be patient and He will enter within ... when you
open yourself to the Lord!!

Chapter I

"Looking up into the heavens"

A Death

Sometimes in life, a death occurs, just happens abruptly. You might have reflected upon the death and asked why did this have to happen? You may have attributed it to a physical, emotional, or material cause that helped you grasp, understand, and accept the reason for this event.

That was not enough to satisfy my wavering curiosities when death first took my mother, then nine months later my father, and the following year my young brother-in-law. At the last funeral, I finally probed the priest who had supported my family through the three deaths as to, "Why did God take away this young man, leaving my sister with two small children?" He responded, "Now, that is the big question!" I thought: That was it? Isn't there more? Why? Why? Why?

When I lost my parents, I looked for guidance in the Bible. The first Bible verse that I was drawn to was the Lord's covenant with Abram, "Look up at the sky and count the stars, if you can." (Genesis

15:5). So often I would look at the stars to remember my mom and dad, and tell them that I missed them. Every evening, if the skies were clear, they would look out their bedroom window and gaze at their "special" star. They had made a pact that it would be their way of communicating with each other when one of them would die. I vividly remember the scene of my parents passing. During their last breaths, they opened their eyes that sparkled, as if they were seeing God, and He was looking out at us.

"My dwelling, like a shepherd's tent, is struck down and borne away from me; You have folded up my life, like a weaver who severs the last thread." (Isaiah 38:12).

God has a plan that is not subject to human whims. Divine Blessings can be relied upon and upon this we must learn to trust.

He Has Come!!!

Sitting ... alone in the darkness ... like being in the
warmth of a womb
Comfort ... safe ... no fears
The flicker of the sanctuary light ...
red warmth, a glow upon my soul.

As I drink in the Love of the Holy Spirit and then ...
The words flow through the pen in my hand ...
written with speed,
from a source deep within.

The Holy Spirit envelopes, caresses, guides,
And directs the written words to be shared ...
Supplying mother's milk ...
flowing from the breast of the Holy Spirit
Nourishing for spiritual growth within my soul ...
where God abides.

And I succumb to His wishes ...
To share with anyone who wants to read or hear.
He offers Himself to those ...
who open themselves in Communion

Gone ... within Him ... and He within you ...
Oh Sweet Lord ... Love ... Peace ...
He has come!!!

Chapter II

"Baby's breath with a rose of new found love"

A Death ... of love

After my parents' deaths, I spent a lot of time focusing on what was important to me in my life. At that time, and thinking over the long term, I was involved in a very unhappy marriage. I prayed to God for guidance and resolve and went for counseling. In the end, the marriage was dissolved and I continued on. I started attending Mass and sought the advice of the parish priest in returning to Catholicism. Another death ... yet the birth of a new life!

Unbeknownst to me, I was being led on a journey. Now that I reflect back, I had traveled through a lot of valleys. Years later, I would discover my development of trust and a love affair with the Leader of my journey, the Lord. I would also find that pieces of events, coincidences, or happenings had "connected" meanings through the Lord.

Trust in God's Help

Lord, please ease my troubled heart,
… For only You know what dwells deep within.
My heart cries out for Your consolation,
… For only You have the true healing powers.
My soul begs for your strength and stability,
… As only Your guidance can provide.

Sadness is like death, a void,
an absence of You, Lord.
Why must I feel like this, when
I love You so much Lord?
The agony of sadness, just as the ecstasy of
happiness that I experience with You,
… Neither can be described.

Such a tug of war is tearing my heart,
… As if the devil is at one end and I at the other or
… Is it You Lord, holding onto my life-line for me?

My comfort is only in You, Lord.
If my tears would only be able to come forth
… Such a release it would be.

When I hear the sweet music of Your Voice, Lord
… Calling me, wanting me to come,
The weight of my sadness and
despair are heavy on my feet,
… Slowing my pace, my nearing to You, Lord.

I felt Your Arms around me this morning Lord,
and I pray for Your continued Embrace.
I love You Lord!!! I want You so much!!!
Lord, I trust You and know that You are with me,
... And I accept whatever crosses,
You wish for me to bear.
I will continue to pray for Your
Guidance and Inspiration.

Sometimes people have a cross to bear, and depending on what it is and our inner strengths and beliefs, determine how we choose its effect on us; how we carry it (or not?) and how (or if?) we survive through it.

Remember that Christ had help in carrying His Cross to His Death. He is teaching us that we must sometimes allow others or Himself to help us through our "cross" bearing times also. And yes, we will falter and fall as He did. But again, Christ shows us, that through our perseverance and trust in Him, we will be saved!

A Lost Love … A Found Love

A lost love …
Will it become a love regained?
Or is it lost forever?

It may be gone … but to another
And this may be the mystery of
what happened to me.
Or … was it a love … ever?

Perhaps it was a weak love,
Which like a chain,
… Was only as strong as its weakest link.

For love on earth
Is not the same as love made in heaven
… And this is what I have for Thee, Lord.

My heart and soul are totally
consumed in You, Lord,
So much, that it is difficult to experience
an earthly love … unless
That spiritual love is truly present …
the strongest link,
Necessary to provide lasting love, of which,
The only love is the love I have for You, Lord.

Mary's total commitment was to only You, Lord.
What else can one compare human love to?
For Christ, Who is the Incarnate,
Could understand human aspect of love,

Yet His was of Divine Love, God.
His Love is limitless, unrestricted ...
But I am human with the
imperfection of limitations
And cannot be so free ... other than with You, Lord.
And ... that is my life's commitment.

Lord, I am Yours only,
And I cannot stray from these feelings.
I have prayed for Your Guidance on my love
And I have no other choice it seems
... total commitment to You.

Lord,
My heart and soul
Mind and body
Human and spiritual ... I am Yours.
You are my love, my only love, Lord
I am totally immersed within You,
... and You in me.

A Bird in a Cage

Sometimes I feel like a bird in a cage
... That needs to be set free.
Lord, please let me spread my wings
... And fly with Thee.

The bars of the cage make it seem
like there is no escape
... Like a damper, a candle snuffer
... Robbing my soul of Your Love and Fire.

Lord, I opened the door to You and now
I am asking You to open the door for me
... To tear down those bars ... so that I may come in.

The door's lock requires the key from Your Heart
... Which is beating within me.
... For it is Your Presence I hunger
Your Heart aches within me.

My home is this cage, Lord
... And the snuffer dwells within it
Lurking, waiting to descend upon my flame
... To extinguish it ... stopping the Heartbeat of Life
And plunging my soul into darkness.

There is no life or living ... without You!

Chapter III

"Providing the beacon of guidance"

A Priest

Once I was "out of my cage," I tried to reassemble my life and reprioritize where and what I would do next. I decided to revisit the parish priest, Father Thomas Cebula, who was so dedicated to my family's needs during the funerals. He seemed so caring and was a good listener, so I made an appointment with him. This turned out to be quite an experience, might I say a change of direction ... up out of the hollow! With his guidance, some of my new found friends and I attended a Cursillo, a women's weekend retreat, and oh my!!! This is what happened next!!!

> *"Thomas said to him, 'Master, we do not know where you are going; how can we know the way?' Jesus said to him, 'I am the way and the truth and the life. No one comes to the Father except through me. If you know me, then you will also know my Father. From now on you do know him and have seen him.' " (John 14:5-7).*

Reflections on a Priest

I can understand how a priest
can be married to only God,
To carry out His Will in such a manner of ministry ...
Unless he has an earthly partner
Who fully understands his commitment to the Lord.

For total commitment,
One must be free of earthly restrictions and ...
Independent to reach out and give to others
Without fear of retribution.

Then those longing for the Lord
Can connect through His Minister
 His Apostle on earth.
And sometimes he may be the only link whom ...
They may experience and then perceive.

Sometimes a priest may be an intermittent link
Offering reaffirmation of others' beliefs or ...
He may be a passing connection
Sowing the seeds of faith
and allowing the rest to the Lord.

One's soul passes through phases ...
From that initial contact ... to total commitment
From nothingness ... to everything wonderful!

But even then ...
A longing may persist for the heavenly-earthly,
human-God connection ...

To fulfill a human desire of spirituality in Our Lord.
A support ... a supporter
To give and receive in love, faith
and hope in God's Virtues ...
To strengthen one's ties with the
Lord and fulfill needs.

Christ our Incarnate is that connection and also ...
A priest so intimately committed to the Lord ...
During his mortal journey on earth.

> *In speaking to Thomas ... Jesus said to him, "Have you come to believe because you have seen me? Blessed are those who have not seen and have believed." (John 20:29).*

My Witness to you ...

It is funny how the Lord works within us.
I have always felt that it was difficult for me to talk about something
that I feel or believe deep within my soul.

When I prayed, God had told me repeatedly
that there will be a time for me
to share my feelings.
He has guided me to share <u>with</u> <u>you</u>,
my spiritual enlightenment.
So as the song goes ... **"Here I am Lord."**

After praying to God for His
Guidance and Inspiration,
my journey unfolded during my Cursillo.
(Women's retreat)
The Cursillo provided a protective "womb,"
an environment for spiritual nurturing,
growth and enlightenment.

You could **really feel** the presence of the Holy
Spirit, working in and among us all.
Presentations provoked spiritual self-examination,
sometimes piercing right into some <u>tender</u>, <u>not</u> <u>so</u>
comfortable areas,
and sometimes providing uplifting
and humorous moments.

Some of us found talents that we didn't even know
we had, but as a group,

we knew we had each other
to complete and complement
whatever God had in store for us.

Not to sound repetitious, but rather to ponder,
<u>these</u> are some of the themes or messages that
affected me spiritually.
I am sure they were heard by all,
but God lets us take these messages, <u>internalize
and personalize</u> them,
to <u>meet our needs</u> and fit them into the "puzzle,"
God's Plan for us, our ideal and purpose for living.
This is done with His Guidance, but <u>only by our</u>
own free will.

Many messages were shared with the group over
those three days at the Cursillo.
I would like to share with you a few of those that
are close to me.

The first message that I would like to share with
you is from Mathew 25:30:

> **"And behold I am with you always."**
> **Say yes to God – and He will not abandon me**
> **and be my friend.**
> **Listen and I will hear Him.**

How many times in the past have I forgotten, just
by second nature,
to try to handle problems or challenges by myself?

I know that I have spent countless hours of fretting or worrying,
when the simple solution was to **hand the problems over to God**,
in <u>pure</u> <u>faith</u> <u>and</u> <u>trust</u>.
<u>This</u> <u>really</u> <u>does</u> <u>work</u>!!

God is with me always.

He is with me in everything I sense:
The sights of nature's beauty
The sounds of people's voices
Touching people, animals, and the Eucharist
Smelling the flowers, home-cooked meals, and the incense of Consecration
Feeling the breeze on my face and the sun's warmth on my body
and writing these ideas to share with you!
I could go on and on ...

But, the most <u>piercing</u>, <u>heart</u> <u>rendering</u> message,
the second message I would like to share with you is from the Book of Revelation 3:20:

"Behold, I stand at the door and knock,
If anyone hears my voice and opens the door,
I will enter his house and dine with him and he with me."

God is at my door.

When I think about my relationship with God, there
is a door between us.
The surprising fact was that **the** handle **to the door
is only on my side**.
<u>Therefore</u>, <u>I must</u> <u>open</u> <u>this</u> <u>door</u> <u>to</u>
<u>allow</u> <u>God</u> <u>to</u> <u>enter</u>.
That door was opened upon my Baptism and
remained open for the next twenty years.
Sometimes though, this door would swing <u>wide
open</u> and other times, <u>just</u> <u>remain</u> <u>ajar</u>
all according to **my choice**.
This well oiled door from Baptism reflected the
innocence of my infancy,
neither knowing right nor wrong with any intention
of sinning.
I guess I could say my key ring contained the first
key, the <u>master</u> <u>key</u> of **'Baptism'**
unlocking the door and allowing it as I has said,
a well oiled door to open widely to God.

In grade school at St. Barbara's, I accepted God's
life in me as **'Grace,'**
that became another key in my collection.
The door pretty much remained open, with the
assistance of more keys:
'Prayer, Penance, and Reconciliation.'
An occasional creak, created by sins, would result
from the trials of growing up
… after all, we aren't perfect.
Soon, another important key was added called,
'Holy Eucharist,'

keeping my heart and soul's door wide open to
receive the Lord.

My spiritual life was still immature and during this
time, I had a strong desire to become a nun. During
the 1960's, I attended Central Catholic High School.
The School, the Church, and I were experiencing **a
lot of changes**, so my idea of becoming a nun got
tucked away and ignored.
My door remained open as in the past.
Then with college and dating,
I started to spiritually weaken,
and my door started to close on God ...
without my realizing what
I was doing to Him or myself.
Oh yes, I had good intentions,
but good intentions without God do not go very far.

In 1971, I married and shortly thereafter, attending
Church became a thing of the past. I kept making
excuses - such as all these changes with the Church
and other personal reasons that at the time -
seemed like good excuses to me.
I needed stability in my life because I didn't have it
personally or find it at Church either.
So why bother? - At least I thought.
The backward slide had begun, the door went shut,
and I had done it.
I closed the door on the Lord <u>for</u> <u>25</u> <u>years</u> without
even thinking.

Looking back now, which they say hindsight is
always 20/20; I wasn't looking to Christ or God.
I was looking <u>inside</u> <u>myself,</u> <u>without</u> <u>God</u>.
The door was closed, and I did it of my own choice.
Once in awhile, there would be a little tweak
of guilt, but that passed quickly ... and the door
started to get rusty with cobwebs
of sin building up around it.
In fact, it was getting pretty <u>dark</u> <u>in</u> <u>my</u> <u>little</u> <u>self-
centered</u> <u>room</u>.
**But ... God was patiently waiting for me, on the
other side of that door**.

Years passed like pages flipping through a book,
and the door remained closed. During these years,
a family member's health suffered and I would
pray to God, even bargain with Him to the point
of hoping that God would give me the illness and
pain, if it had to exist. One night I even called a
TV prayer-line, desperate, **but** still it was **only me,
knocking on my side** of the door, **again** asking for
favors, not really opening it.
I had **shut that door and locked it so securely**.
<u>Maybe</u>, I was kind of fumbling around then?
Looking for my keys?
Time went on and my parents passed away. Both
times these crises arose, **for some reason**, I tried to
make sure that **their** spiritual needs were fulfilled
on their deathbeds. Again, this happened with the
death of my young brother-in-law.
I even survived a serious auto accident and falling
off a roof, and always in the **back of my mind**, I had

this **"feeling"** that maybe God, for **some reason**, wanted me to survive without harm.

Another mystery to me occurred that following year. I got the "itch" to start reading the Bible. I started on my own, and really got the bug to find out more about the background of the Bible times, people, and cultures, to better understand it. I started to make connections of references of what people wrote then with what Christ did in the New Testament.

I started keeping a diary.

I guess I was kind of **peeking** through a crack in the door boards

and seeing some light that was trying to come in, **especially those stars** that God talked about so much in the Old Testament.

I joined the neighborhood Bible study. I considered it lightly as <u>just</u> <u>a</u> <u>bunch</u> <u>of</u> <u>women</u> who got together and were studying the Book of John.

Then **suddenly**, I felt driven, with a strange curiosity, to go visit a priest, who just happened to be Father Thomas Cebula. I wanted to see if I could even get back into the Catholic Church. I assumed that it would take an

act of God to get me accepted.

In fact, **God's Plan was acting on me, really working with me**, naïve as I still was.

Remember my feelings of "for some reason," "itches," and "curiosity?"

I thought, oh I'll start going to Church,

But that's it - no extras - so I thought.

God was knocking on my door, and
He had plans for me.
I was so <u>readily</u> and <u>lovingly</u> accepted back to the
Church ... that I couldn't believe it!

Quick!!
Grab that can of oil -
Grease up those hinges with graces,
Shovel out those piles of excuses,
Dust out the cobwebs of sins and **add** some prayer
for polish!

I found my keys of **'Reconciliation'**
and **'Holy Eucharist,'**
opened the door - **and in came God - full force!!!**
I **grabbed onto Him** and have been
on the ride of my life ever since!
The door is **really wide open!**

His blessings and graces keep showering upon me,
taking me to unbelievable heights!!
This prodigal daughter returned to a
<u>warm</u> <u>and</u> <u>caring</u> Father,
Who gave me a big hug and welcome back - and a
banquet that is still going on!
I don't ever want it to end!!

Remember the girl who didn't want to be involved?
Well God continues to work His Plan
out with her as I write.
She is a Eucharistic Minister, Lector, in a Spiritual
Group, and keeps her heart open for more.

And remember the old neighborhood Bible Study group? After a long absence, I returned to find the group studying about the reading from Revelations 3:20: "... **If anyone hears my voice and opens the door...**"
I Got Your Message Lord!!!
Listen and the Lord will speak to you!

There were so many important messages that I heard at the Cursillo/retreat that I need to add one last, but not least, message that is held very close to my heart:

The Cursillo Formula:

Make a friend
Be a friend
Talk to Jesus about your friend
Talk to your friend about Jesus.

I had followed this formula without even being aware of its existence. Father Tom Cebula had been a friend I made through all the family crises. His dedication, genuine caring, and spirituality also inspired me in my decision to come back to the Church. He and the Lord guided me back onto God's pathway without my ever knowing. This is so true. I have since, talked many times to Father about my spiritual friendship with the Lord, and to the Lord about my spiritual mentoring friendship with Father Tom.

The door has been re-opened and the foundation laid with my love, faith and trust in the Lord.

The Lord's warmth is firming and setting my spiritual mortar through His Graces.

I continuously reinforce it with prayers.

Now, I can add windows, open them up, and share my blessed happiness and message with others. It is:

Jesus,
A deep feeling of thirst, quenched by Your Blood
A pit of hunger, filled by Your Body
Total refreshment in You, Lord,
Inspiring, uplifting my soul.

The colors, such as the beauty of God's gift
to us in nature
How could my eyes want for more,
other than You, Lord?
The love and passion, caring and sharing
How can I feel so empty,
unfilled but without You, Lord?
Never satisfied until You fill me up.

Talking to You, and with You
Hearing and feeling You in me
Move me, stir me, and do with me as You want.
Your desire is my desire.
Guide me, my feet will follow. I give You my feet.
My hands, my senses, my body and soul
Use them all up until they cannot be used anymore.

Then, take me into Your Loving Arms, Lord
And hold me forever.
I love You, Lord!!

**May God's Grace, Peace and Warmth be with you!
De Colores!!!**

So must all love be
Of many bright colors
To make my heart cry.

The Opened Treasure Chest

It is as if within me
there is a little treasure chest
waiting to be opened
... and only You have the key Lord.

A small locket perhaps
maybe it is my heart, or my soul
that awaits Your arrival
to be opened up.

You came Lord, and unlocked my heart,
As I had been anxiously awaiting and anticipating.
The time drew near and You came closer and closer
Until ... it happened!!

The chest was opened.
A sudden burst of air escaped from within me,
and a vacuum was created
that allowed You to enter.

As I desperately inhaled Your Sweetness,
the Splendor of Your Golden Glory
... poured into me ... flowing like rivers,
the rapids of my baptism renewed.

My soul was delivered into Your
Shimmering Presence
... suspended in Your Mercy and Love
... forevermore.

Pure white, shimmering lights surround me,
... sparkling, pleasing, and safely welcoming me.

Lord ... You are simple ... yet complex.
I can see You Lord in Your Presence,
... not through my eyes, but inside my heart,
... open to You, Lord.

Returning to the Lord

Lord,
You will never scorn my love,
As You will my sins.

But Your unspoken Forgiveness is felt.
The weight is lifted from my soul
... allowing me to breathe without effort,
... while the Holy Spirit pours
into me with each inspiration,
... feeding my body, my soul ... inspiring me,
Bringing me ever, so much closer to You.

The flame is lit, blazing within my heart.
Feel the warmth radiated from me
... as you touch my hands, my face,
... and embrace me.

Then ... we breathe as one ...
spiritually united with You!!!
I am home again, home with You, Lord
... and I Love You!!!

The Lord said:
"I am here, but you do not see Me.
As I lift you up on the waves of My Love ... you drift
closer to Me,
And as you turn your sails to My Winds,
My Hands guide your vessel ... into My Heart."
"There you will feel my True Love and Rapture

In My Brightness of Life-giving Love and Warmth
... only we can share."

"Your vessel is within Me ... as you receive Me
in the Eucharist.
You totally surrender to Me ...
And we are consumed in Oneness."

Chapter IV

"Life emerges from the woven cocoon"

A Weaver

Deaths and divorce, sprinkled with unhappi-ness, doubts, and unanswered questions, had fragmented my life. My journey had woven through tumultuous times living in darkness, but now is in the Light. I allowed the Lord, through the priest, my spiritual mentor, to re-weave my life back together with my God-given golden thread. I opened myself to the Lord and gave Him control through prayer and contemplation, and in receiving the Holy Eucharist. **Life is good!!**

As my Bridegroom in heaven waits for me, He has blessed me with Douglas, a wonderful, loving bride-groom on earth, who also opens himself to the Lord.

Gifts continue to be added to my spiritual weaving as my life of black and white is brightened with the colors of God's Gifts and Blessings. These gifts, I wish to share with you. And as you read, may your life be woven closer to the Lord as ... **You open yourself to the Lord!!**

Spiritual weaving, tensiled with God's Love and Gifts will withstand the strains of earthly life!

"The veil was woven of violet, purple and scarlet yarn, and of fine linen twined, with cherubim embroidered on it. The curtain for the entrance of the tent was made of violet, purple and scarlet yarn, and of fine linen twined, woven in a variegated manner." (Exodus 36:35, 37).

The Golden Thread

A thread, a golden thread
... The thread of one's soul to be spun by the Lord,
... Before He breathes life into it.

It is a thread, of the purest gold, perfect
... Worthy only of and from the Lord
Molded into the soul, to connect with life
... Upon the consummation of His Love,
... Shared between two lovers.
And, the love became Life with His Breath
... As He placed His Blessing
upon their joined bodies.
And, He smiled upon the conception.

The golden thread became a human life
... With a beating heart,
Nurtured through the thread of a mother
... The umbilical thread of life.

The little life came from the womb
And the golden thread was washed with the waters
of Baptism
... Becoming clean and shiny
... Waiting to be spun into a golden treasure,
... As part of a vessel of the Lord.
And, the Lord dwelled within
the golden threaded vessel.

The golden thread was nurtured, bathed,
... And laden heavily with Christ's Body and Blood.

Each layer of golden thread was
enriched and strengthened
... With Gifts of Gold bestowed from the Holy Spirit.

And the golden thread travelled
through the eyelets of time,
... Wandering to and fro, weaving
its way along its journey.
As God guided each stitch of the thread,
... It weathered the times,
... Sometimes hidden in the pockets of gatherings,
... And other times, outstanding, shining brightly ...
for all to behold.

And as time passed,
... The thread endured the trials
of pulling ... and knots.
But, God was always there,
... To soothe and smooth the snags of time.
Sometimes, the thread was tense enough to break.
... But in being made of the soft, pliable gold as God
had designed,
... The thread withstood and grew with the Love of
the Lord and His Gifts.

The thread may become entwined with the golden
thread of another,
... Reaching for God's Hand and His approval
... To begin yet another pattern,
creating another strand
... Making the Lord smile.

Or...
The thread may travel without entanglement
... Helping other golden threads become
untarnished and re-polished
... Making the Lord smile.

As the golden thread was nearing
the end of its journey,
... The Lord looked upon what He had sewn with
this golden thread.
... And He smiled as He looked upon His Work.
... He was pleased.

For the love He had created was a Heart of Gold,
... A soul that Christ dwelt within,
sitting on His Golden Throne.
... And He was pleased.

So the golden thread remained in God's Hands
... And enwrapped within His Heart ... so closely
... That it melted in the Heat, the Flame of His Love,
And ... became the shining, treasured golden love
of His Heart.

Chapter V

"Ice Angel on Onondaga Lake"

Mary, Mother of Jesus

Many times, I would reflect on Mary and never know quite what I could say to her. She was so beautiful. Although, I never had children, I often tried to visualize, feel what it would have been like to experience being the Mother of Jesus. The wonder of knowing her Blessed Honor, yet the horrid events that culminated in the death of Her Son. A mother's hope dashed, resulting in such a miraculous, joyous rising! Deep in her heart, pierced with such pain, the Holy Spirit caressed her sorrow, bathing her with the graces and love, strengthening her will, faith, and trust in that, this was God's will ... to save mankind.

Believe and have faith in Him, allow Him to caress you, and you will live.

Reflection on the Hail Mary ...

When praying your Rosary today Mary, my heart, my soul were deeply pondering your words, and the Lord, through His Heart within me, inspired me to ponder even further into writing reflections of your prayer.

I am not really sure where this may lead, but as always, I open myself to You, Lord, and You will guide my heart, soul and mind, to my fingertips, to open whatever is your message ... so Mary, I open myself to you, to share your message.

I have been guided to use your Prayer, the Hail Mary, and so I have written it out in English and Latin, of which I am not very knowledgeable, to get the full richness of your message. Therefore, I am yours, as I am of your Son, His Bride. Dear Mother, whatever it takes ... my trust is in you.

"In the sixth month, the angel Gabriel was sent from God to a town in Galilee called Nazareth, to a virgin betrothed to a man named Joseph, of the House of David, and the virgin's name was Mary. And coming to her, he said, 'Hail, favored one! The Lord is with you.' " (Luke 1:26-28).

Hail Mary
Full of Grace
The Lord is with Thee
Blessed are Thou amongst women
And Blessed is the Fruit of Thy Womb
Jesus

Holy Mary
Mother of God
Pray for us sinners
Now and at the hour of our death
Amen

Ave Maria - Hail Mary
Gratia Plena - Full of Grace
Dominus tecum - The Lord is with you
Benedicta tu - O how blest are you
In mulieribus - Among earth's women
Et Benedictus Fructus ventris tui - And how truly
blest is the Fruit of your womb Jesus
Sancta Maria - O Holy Mary
Mater Dei - God's own Mother
Ora pro nobis - Pray for us
Pecca toribus - Your children who stray
from the way
Nunc et in hora mortis nostrae - Now and in that
final hour
Amen

Hail Mary!

Well, Mary, what else could be more fitting than to call all of our attention to you, our focus upon you, since you are the Mother of Our Lord. You deem honor in your blessed role of Mother Mary, "Mary", such a pure name, as you were a virgin. I know very little about your life, but I feel that that is about to change, and I am not certain why.

I feel an innocence, a purity within me when I think of you, gentle, loving, caring, yet a strength in you, especially when you said "Yes" to God. You had no fear, and I wonder if you could grasp the importance of your decision at the time, especially what you would have to experience in the end ... His Pain, Suffering and Death.

But being an earthly person, you allowed your faith in the Lord, an acceptance of trust, allowing the Holy Spirit to dwell within you, resulting in the conception of Our Lord, a miracle indeed!

Hail, a miracle within you, Mary!!
A blessed event, you are Blessed and deserving of
our Hail,
Our honor to you, from whom the
Lord Jesus came ...
To save us!

"Mary said, 'Behold I am the handmaid of the Lord. May it be done to me according to your word.' Then the angel departed from her." (Luke 1:38).

Full of Grace …

You were filled by the Holy Spirit. But more than that, you were filled with the Trinity. You were praying to God, Our Creator, Our Father, and He answered you by showering you with His Graces, through the Holy Spirit, and then rested within you in conceiving His Son, Jesus. You were filled with the Presence of Graces, the Trinity, all Three within One, within you!! What a wonderful experience to turn to Lord and receive Him spiritually and physically. A communion, you were succumbed, and your consummation culminated in a miraculous conception, the Lord Jesus, within your womb. Oh God, what wonder!!

Lord, I feel so close to You, and especially with the thoughts of when I receive Your Body and Blood. I become totally consumed in Your Love and as Your Bride, I succumb to Your Desires and Wishes, just as Mary did, when she said "Yes!"... as I do now. Opening totally to You, for You to dwell within me, as You are, because … You have given me Your Heart beating within my bosom, just as You gave Your Son to Mary within her womb. And I love You for that, Lord. As a mother loves her child, Mary loved Jesus … and as Jesus' Bride, I love You and will treasure Your Heart forever!!

How can one be any fuller of Grace? My graces from You, Lord, are so wonderful and pleasing, that I desire You much more, and want to share You with others … who open their hearts and souls to You too. To have Your Graces, Lord, just as Mary, I am so thankful and graciously am Yours. You have my heart and soul, my being, just as You have Mary's committed to You, and ... we will be forever consumed within each other. My soul lives forever in Your Graces.

Mary, full of Grace, full of the Lord,
May anyone who opens themselves up to Your
Son, be filled with the Lord's Graces,
As their hearts and souls turn to you, in
seeking Our Lord.

The Lord is with Thee ...

Oh Mary, the Lord came to you, and you took Him in - total acceptance, surrender, in total faith and trust, a commitment to whatever His Plan would be for you, for His Son, and for all of mankind. You accepted God's Plan for the future of man's spirituality, our Salvation. You bore the Lord's Saving Grace, our Destiny. You were His Temple, His Vessel, what a strong spiritual woman - totally unselfish, because you gave to us, our way of Salvation, through your Blessed Womb, in which you bore the Son of God.

What a wonderful feeling it must have been, to physically experience the Baby Jesus within You, feeling His Movements within your body, and then to be able to bear the Child of God, His Son, laboring and then nursing Him from your breasts, a motherly, spiritual, and physical bond. The Lord was within you, dependent upon you, as we depend upon Him, to suckle upon His Love. He nurses our souls with His Graces, providing us with precious life-giving milk, like mother's milk, nourishing our hearts and souls, giving unselfishly, a bonding with us, as you were on earth with Him, and are now in Heaven.

The Lord was with you then and you remain with
Him in Heaven,
The Lord is with Thee.
The Lord is with anyone, who opens themselves to
Him, as you did
... And that is His Promise.

"Then the angel said to her, 'Do not be afraid, Mary, for you have found favor with God. Behold, you will conceive on your womb and bear a son, and you shall name him Jesus.' " (Luke 1:30-31).

Blessed are Thou amongst women ...

To be chosen, selected by the Lord, among all the women of time, such an honor, a blessing and for this, you are above all, even as one in human, yet now divine. You remain among us, with a Mother's arms, waiting to welcome, to hold, just as you held your Son, Jesus. You are blessed in conceiving, bearing, raising, and dying within the Lord, and the Lord within you.

You, in your humility, exemplified love, an undying love, in which we all should take to our hearts and then share with others. Your heart suffered many sorrows to the depths of despair, when your Son was nailed to the Cross, with each blow of the scourging and with each nail placed into your Son's Body; a sword pierced your heart, just as they pierced Christ's Body.

But now, your heart is wrapped, enraptured in the ecstasy of the Lord in Heaven, where you inspire hope for the hopeless and love for the unloved.

You, among us, are blessed and
provide as a mother
Whenever God's children pray in your name.

And Blessed is the Fruit of Thy Womb ...

Mary, you bore the Blessed Seed, within the rich fertile flesh of your womb, and here your blood became His Blood, and your flesh became His flesh. You provided humanity to our Spiritual, Divine Deity, Jesus, the Incarnation, and the Fruit of your womb Mary, our Savior.

Your virgin womb provided a pure, sinless, perfect, warm, and nurturing environment for a Perfect Human, Our Lord. You were free from original sin, so the seed of the Lord, whom you bore, was the Perfect, Blessed Fruit of your pure womb.

Mary, your Fruit, as a Gift to you and to mankind, was the succulent Fruit of Our Lord and as we partake in the Fruit of Jesus, in our Baptism, we are freed from original sin which resulted from the enjoyment of the forbidden fruit. The Blessed Fruit frees us from the evils of the banned fruit. A Fruit from within the pure and sinless, nourishes the heart and soul weakened by evil, original sin, giving us Life and Promise ... from the Blessed Fruit of your womb, Jesus Christ.

Our bodies, as vessels of the Lord, become the womb of our souls and God gives us His Graces, His Fruits, to become a part of our souls. Within the wombs of our bodies, our souls are nourished and grow, bearing fruits, graciously labored, freely molded, as we desire of God's Desires.

Mary, as you freely chose and accepted to bear the Seed of Our Lord within your womb; I freely accept the Seed of His Fruits and Graces, within my womb, my body. Out of my womb, through the labor of my love for the Lord, may I deliver my heart and soul in the Spirit of Christ's Love, a time for celebration and sharing. May the blessing of the fruits of my womb be as worthy to the Lord as the Blessed Fruit of your womb, Jesus.

The love of your labor was the Blessed Fruit of your womb, Jesus, closeness between two, which cannot be other than of God and man, and their love for each other, a birth of Life and Love, the Lord, for us and within us.

**We eat of Your Fruit Lord, our Blessed Communion,
The Fruit from You and Your Mother, Mary.**

Jesus ...

Oh Jesus, You are the Grace, the Fruit that dwelt within Mary, and now within me, and anyone who accepts You as their Savior. You are the Lord, who came to us, the Word Incarnate, Man, Son of God, the human connection, God to man. To understand man, God became Man, Jesus, and therefore to understand God, Jesus must dwell within us and enrich us with Himself.

He gave us Himself by becoming Man through Mary and now we receive Him, His Body and Blood, since Mary accepted, giving of herself, her human-ness, so that we may receive Him.

Jesus blessed Mary, and blessed motherhood, by becoming man through a woman, and blessed the family bond, the marriage of a man and woman. You brought the Trinity to us in Flesh and Blood, of our bodies, and then blessed the human body by resurrecting it from the dead and consecrating it to Godliness, by raising Your Body and Your Mother Mary's to perfection, Your Dwelling Place in Heaven.

You blessed the essence of human flesh, not only by creating it in Your Image, but by taking the human body as Your Dwelling Place during Your stay here on earth and continue on in each of our own bodies, as Your Temples, until we die and are resurrected upon Your return.

Jesus, the Incarnate, through Your
Conception in Mary,
One in Perfect Communion, as we are ... I am ...
Whenever I open myself to You and receive
You in Communion.

Holy Mary ...

Mary, sanctified by God by bearing His Son, Jesus, and the Lord raised you up above all others. Such an honor it was to be chosen to bear and give birth, to Our Savior.

Your body sanctified, became a Temple of the Lord in a way, that no other human can be, but you have shown us that our bodies too, may serve as Temples in keeping the Love of Our Lord within, just as you did, in believing, accepting, and then giving birth, to give us a promise of eternal life.

Holy Mary, You not only gave birth to Your Savior, Our Savior, but you gave us all the Life of Christ. You allowed it to happen from the moment of your encounter with the Holy Spirit, to the horrific death of Your Son, God's Son ... you allowed it. You could have rejected your role as Mother, but you trusted the Lord, just as you are teaching us to do the same.

Your motherly love was set in a profound foundation of trust and faith in the Lord that you did not interfere, rather allowing, submitting to God's complete control of your life, despite the extraordinary pains that you endured in watching your Son's Suffering and Death.

You gave us the holiness of motherhood, sisterhood, and love, unselfishly displayed, shared. A comforting love, that only a mother can give ... a humble love ... a holy love.

Your holiness, sacredness, and sanctity were rewarded in the Lord's raising you to Heaven, to be with Him, just as we shall be, if ... we follow your guidance. You give so much love and comfort to so many, in all ways of life. You are an inspiration for all.

The Holiness of God is still shared through your intercession today,
As we honor you,
Holy Mary.

Mother of God ...

Mother of God, Oh Mary, such an honor for a woman, especially one so meek, so mild, so humble. You shine of courage and inspiration for those who are contemplating the motherly nature, which applies in so many ways. A mother's love can be shared in one's life in many ways, whether a woman is a mother or childless. You reach into anyone's heart, which opens up to you.

Such a powerful role, a wonderful, inspiring role, it is to be the Mother of God. It is hard to imagine the awesomeness of your Miraculous Conception. To be the Mother of Jesus, of God - it is hard to fathom, but you accepted and fulfilled what all women would desire.

God as our Creator, Creator of life, Father, Abba, touched us so intimately by sending the Holy Spirit to dwell upon you, within you, and brought forth His Son, Jesus, all Three in One, within you, Mother of God. You gave birth to His Son, Who is Our Brother, from His Father, Our Father, so we look to you as Our Mother too.

As Mother of God, Our Lord Jesus, you provide strength and courage to mothers who experience the illness, separation, and the loss of their children, but you have also blessed the human bond, the motherly love with her child. As God turned to you, to be the Mother of His Son, Jesus Christ, may others turn to you in such confidence and love, knowing that you accept them and love them, and will say "Yes" to them, just as you did to Our Father, Your Father, Christ's Father, God.

As Mother of God, you are an inspiration
for all children,
To seek their mother's love, trust, and guidance,
Because they know that a mother's love for her
children never dies,
And yet ... she allows God to take her children by
His Hand to walk beside,
Mother and child ... on their journey
with and to Him.

"And the angel said to her in reply, 'The holy Spirit will come upon you, and the power of the Most High will over shadow you. Therefore the child born will be called holy, the Son of God.'" (Luke 1:35).

Pray for us sinners ...

Mary, how many times I never think to ask of your prayers, for your intercessions, when asking for the Lord's Forgiveness and Favors. In your motherly love, you are dedicated to helping your children, the Children of God, in their times of trials, of sins, to reach out to the Lord and obtain His Blessings.

You never abandon us, just as you never abandoned Your Son, Jesus, as He faced the trial for His Life, His Beliefs, and for us. You, who can only comfort as a mother can, are here to guide us whenever we ask of you. Just as you dedicated your life, your heart, soul and body to the Lord, many come to you, seeking your blessings upon their lives' choices, whether it is sisterhood, lay life, or matrimony, instilling a special trust upon these bonds or vows, a life-long commitment.

Mary, you are there pick us up when we fall into sin, skinning our souls, to wipe the tears away from our hearts, as we implore forgiveness, and promise not to sin again. "Oh Mother, I promise not to do that again" - how many times we have said, and there you are, our Mother, picking us up and loving us, looking at Our Father and saying "They are sorry they hurt You, Lord, please forgive and forget, please give them another chance." Then you brush us off, give us a hug, and allow us to go on, as a doting mother would ... but always there waiting for whenever we need you, or ask for you.

You prayed for us sinners, when your heart ached within your breast, with the pain of losing

Your Son, as He turned His Face to the evil darkness, You prayed for us sinners, as You allowed Your Son, Jesus Christ, to experience His Suffering Way to the Cross on Calvary, praying for Him, for relief of His Suffering, and His Death, allowing Him to escape from this human agony, atoning for our sins. You prayed for us sinners then, and you continue to do so today.

You, Mary without sin, understand the need for your intercession for us sinners.

Mary, I am a sinner,
Born with sin, cleansed by Baptism,
And have fallen back to sin time and time again.
But as your child, I know I can turn to you for
whatever need I may have.

Now and at the hour of our death ...

When I think of "now", I think of this instant, this moment, now, but "now" is a constraint on time and when praying, I reflect more on God's time. When praying deeply, I submit to God's Desires, not mine, God's Will, not mine. So now, Mary, I pray to you, at this moment, for your intercession, your love, your protection, in your time. I am not asking for your answer now, just for you to turn to me, while I focus my prayers to you for your intercession. Isn't it wonderful that I can pray anytime to you, and to Our Lord, and receive your attentions?

And to have your presence called upon us in our moments of death, such a precious gift you give us. I can call upon you when I face death in its different aspects, such as death of my soul in sin, temptation, or death of my heart in loss of love, caring, whether giving or receiving, death of my spirit in self-rejection or by others, death of a loved one spiritually, mentally or physically, or upon my death, ending my body's existence on earth.

To have you present during my final moments on earth, what a glorious event that would be! To envision You, Mary, with your arms open to guide me, knowing that you will give me to Your Son, Christ, Who is readily at hand, awaiting my soul's return, from where it came.

To have you present during my final moments, knowing this reassures me that together, in your presence, we will share our hearts and souls with the Lord, forever. The last hour will unfold and open into an eternity with God, and then ... we will rejoice in Communion, a Feast in Heaven with Our Lord, the long awaited union, re-union of our hearts, minds, souls ... and then resurrected with celestial bodies, as You and Jesus now share.

Amen.

*And now, Mary, in Your Name, I draw deeper,
more profound, closer to Your Son and
Our Father, through the Holy Spirit's Presence into
a total submission, acceptance and trust ...
to allow God's Power, His Spirit, to dwell within
me, and to fulfill His Desires ...
let it be so, in Christ, my Love ... it is done.
Thank You, God the Father, the Son,
and the Holy Spirit
... And thank you, Mary, our Blessed Mother!!*

Chapter VI

"Sunset, Good Night from Onondaga Lake"

Dreams

One night, I dreamt of a woman dressed in white, standing at an altar, wearing a tiara made of gold. There was two other people standing, one on each side of her, at the altar facing me. She had on a long white gown with flowing sleeves, and her hair was light, but not blonde. I prayed on this and was led to read the Book of Esther. The name Esther is Persian, meaning "star." The theme of stars had again returned in my reading the Bible.

The Dream of Mordecai:

> "This was his dream. There was noise and tumult, thunder and earthquake-confusion upon earth. Two great dragons came on, both poised for combat. They uttered a mighty cry and at their cry every nation prepared for war, to fight against the race of the just. It was a dark and gloomy day. Tribulation and distress, evil and great

confusion, lay upon the earth. The whole race of the just were dismayed with fears of the evils to come upon them, and were at the point of destruction. Then they cried out to God, and as they cried, there appeared to come forth a great river, a flood of water from a little spring. The light of the sun broke forth; the lowly were exalted and they devoured the nobles." (The Book of Esther 1:4-10).

This story, told in Esther, occurred during the feast of Purim (lots) when the lot of destruction of the Jews was reversed into salvation, through the actions of Queen Esther and her uncle, Mordecai. The feast occurs on the 14th and 15th of Adar (February-March).

My dream occurred March 15th. I had never heard of this feast, and I recalled a sermon in which Fr. Tom spoke about an Esther and her leading in the saving of the Jews, but that was all I could remember.

My life of change:

"Of this period of beautifying treatment, six months were spent with oil of myrrh, and the other six months with perfumes and cosmetics ... She could not return to the king unless he was pleased with her and had her summoned by name." (The Book of Esther 2:12, 14).

I realized that I would receive a reward later, if I would have faith and trust. As a Christian, I had to learn to depend upon God's Graces during my times of need. God had chosen me, as He does with all, for a special purpose and ... I felt as "special" as when the king had chosen Esther.

"The king loved Esther more than all other women ... so he placed the royal diadem on her head ... Who knows but that it was for a time like this that you obtained the royal dignity? ... 'If I perish, I perish.'" (The Book of Esther 2:17, 4:14, 16).

In the Chapel:

Just as I had prayed in the Chapel frequently, pleading for God's Guidance, Esther, in her time of needs, had also turned to the Lord:

"Hear my prayer; have pity on my inheritance and turn our sorrow into joy: thus we shall live to sing praise to your name, O Lord. Do not silence those who praise you." (The Book of Esther C: 10).

The Prayer of Esther:

"Save us by your power, and help me, who am alone and have no one but you, O Lord. You know all things. ... From the day I was brought here till now, your handmaiden has had no joy except in you, O lord, God of Abraham. O

God, more powerful than all, hear the voice of those in despair. Save us from the power of the wicked, and deliver me from my fear." (The Book of Esther Chap C: 25, 29).

Here We Are, Lord

Here we are Lord, here we are
In this room, all alone
We dance and embrace each other.
In each other's arms, Oh Lord I'm Yours.

I am floating, I am gliding,
Holding onto to You, Oh Lord.
And as we dance to our beating hearts,
We are one Lord, all alone.

I really love You,
I really love You,
I really love You, with all my heart.

To heaven we'll dance arm in arm.
We will dance the night away.

We belong to one another,
So we will dance the night away.
We are one, eternally Oh Lord,
So please take me away.

As I look into Your Eyes, Lord
My heart is melting and we become one,
Stardust shimmering all around us,
Soft petals of love, pure white light.

I really love You,
I really love You,
I really love You, with all my heart.

We belong to one another
So please take me away.

I really love You,
I really love You,
I really love You, with all my heart.

We belong to one another,
So …. please … take me away!!!

"I saw you, my lord, as an angel of God, and my heart was troubled with fear of your majesty. For you are awesome, my lord, though your glance is full of kindness. As she said this, she fainted." (The Book of Esther Chap D: 13-15).

Chapter VII

"The Sacred Heart of Jesus Christ"

Christ's Sacred Heart

My frequent visits to the Chapel at St. Barbara's offered me many opportunities to experience the Lord in contemplative silence. I prayed for the many "issues" in my life. I relaxed in His Presence, alone, and allowed whatever to transpire. Sometimes I felt peace, other times turmoil, and other times exhilaration, excitement, and "gifts." God's "Gifts" of words would rush into my mind, so I started jotting them in the candlelight. The words would arrive so fast and furious that my writing was a scrambled page. I would run out of space and write all around the margins. Fragments of papers fulfilled their purpose to reflect upon at a later date. I would try to make "sense" of the words sometimes, questioning myself, "Did I really write this?" or "Where did this come from?"

I also signed up for an hour of Adoration of the Blessed Eucharist on the First Friday night shift. It was there that I experienced one of the most spiritual, uplifting, indefinable "Gifts." I felt as if my heart was "encased" by the Christ's Sacred Heart and that His Sacred Heart was actually within me, beating, sustaining my human existence. It was as if my heart was replaced by Christ's Heart. I had opened myself and He was and has remained within me!!!

Your Heart is within Me

Lord,
Your Heart is within me today
Your Gift to me, that I have accepted
And I will love, protect, share and cherish ... as You
Wish.

So special ... so special
I feel different, I have changed
... but uncertain in what way or direction
You are leading me, Lord.

But I know,
Deep in this Heart of Yours ... of mine ...
We are one in each other ... and ...
It is Magnificent, Blessed!
And ... I love You even more!!

You have me and my total being.
So please Lord,
Do as you will
Your Desire is my desire
Your Needs are my needs
Your Love is my love
... and all to share.

I am totally enraptured in You
... there is no separation anymore
... total unity is ours.
I am embraced in Your Heart
... as You revealed to me.

My heart no longer exists
… it is only of You.
I can only live, love, and sense
… through You Lord … and You in I.

We are Lovers, united totally
… and I have no doubt or fear.

I am Yours, Lord
… and … You are mine.
We are one!!
… and … I love You!!!

"Come follow Me," He calls to me
… and I have gone in my heart and soul
… not to return, but to go forward with Him
… in Him and He in me.

I will go out to Him in others
… and we will be one … and one … and one …
In love, heart, mind and soul.

Your Heart beats ever so strongly
… and so full of love
For anyone who may desire of me … of You … Lord!

I Want to be Lost in You Forever

Your Heart Lord, beats within me
... as You open my eyes to the love
    You intended men to share among men.

For love once given and returned,
... is of Your Love, Lord...
From within one ... to within another
    Is of Your Love, Lord.

Your Love begets love.
Your Father begot You in human love, Incarnate
... and remains with us in Your Love, the Spirit ...
so that You are Who Am,
as You said "I Am Who Am."
    All in one, One Love, God.

You flowed within me and ... we became one,
... as I succumbed and accepted Your Love...
... and I returned Yours ...
    And ... this is of You, in Your Image,
    Your Likeness.

You remain within me.
Your Heart ... beating ... beating
... emanating the Spirit,
... becoming Your Life within me ... my soul,
    Abounding in warmth, radiating Light.

Your Love for me to experience ...
and others to behold.

To see and experience You through me,
within me ...
  As I experience You.

I *feel* You ... I *breathe* You
... and I am of You ... for You to behold and be
pleased
  For Your Pleasure Lord ... all for Your Love.

I am bathed in Your Love, Lord
... and Your Heart beats Life through me,
... protected ... beneath my breast.
  I long to hide You within my soul,
  our secret castle.

Alone ... to lavish within each others' love.
Like juices of grapes, the sweetest wine
... we *taste* each other, drinking our love, *lifting* us
up together
  As we rise from the castle of my soul ... to Your
Heavenly Abode.

There is no fluidity between the physical and the
physical, finite.
  But rather a flow between ... the spiritual and
the infinite.

Infinity ... no beginning ... no end ... timelessness.
  Precious spirituality, **the Lord.**

Light has no edge ... for where does it begin?
And ... where does it end?

It is all that is beheld, perceived by the physical eye.
But, its essence flows, such is why...
The Light, The Love is of God!
Something that cannot be defined,
and ... is not defined in physical
terms of the senses.
But, rather is of God, flowing, endless, without
boundaries ... eternal.
   *Without restriction or definition, an awaring
presence of its own.*

My heart, encased within my body,
... longs to burst out from the restriction
of its cage of bones,
... the flesh covering, reinforcing.
But once pierced, allows fluidity,
an expiration of life, air
... just as my heart and soul will become ...
   Upon Your arrival!

You sweep me up Lord!!
I am exhumed from the human, physical constraints
   and I am freed ... to unite with You!

My soul becomes engaged and
consumed within You
... and Your Heart returns to You ...
containing my soul.
My essence of life, fused ...
enmeshed ... engrossed...
   And finally ... absorbed with You!

Perfect Fire, Ablaze!
... as my eyes become fixed upon You.
Like a beacon ... a buzzing ... electrical.

Then ... *hushing sounds ... like crystal ...*
like wind chimes.
You Breathe Life into my soul
... as You bestow upon Your Bride
... the twinkling, sparkling, purity, a coolness,
crispness of purity,
... translucent yet transparent.
> *So inviting ... that I cannot sense enough of it.*

And ... **I want to be lost in You ... forever!**

The Heart That Beats Love

The Heart that beats Love … is within my chest.
His Sacred Heart, a Blessing from Above
My qualms and fears now rest.
My love for You, Lord … will never die.

My thoughts are always of You.
I love You Lord, Jesus!

You are my Husband, my Spouse,
… my Love, my All and … I am Your Bride,
Yours to hold and embrace.
It is for You that I live … and rely upon,
Your Inspiration and Grace.

Your Father, my Father,
Who loves us so much
… deems that we love each other.
My love for Thee is such that
… the Holy Spirit has arrived
… bringing wedding Gifts
… providing the ultimate, unifying Touch.

For You are Three in One,
… we are united … a communion.

My heart has come to You,
… and You have entered within me
… throughout my entirety.
So that … we are immersed within each other
      For eternity!!

Deeper, deeper we fall within each other
... down a tunnel.
And ... we are lost within each other
... nowhere to be found
... until ... the last moment of time.
For then, You will expose to me Lord,
Your Blessed Sight!

You have come to me, for me, my Love
... and I touch Your Hand, gazing into
Your Loving Eyes.
My soul is enraptured, captivated by Your Love
... succumbing to Your Existence
And... we become one within each other ...
    Until the end of time!!

Your bride has welcomed You to be within her.
You have given her Your Heart ...
and taken hers in return.
One cannot live without the other
... so that I no longer exist, only You
... and I am lost in You!!!

Find the Lord ... and you will find me.

Only in Heaven

I hold my hands cupped to my chest
When I open them, I see Your Heart, Lord.
I love You with all my heart.

Within my hands ... I kiss Your Heart
And hold It firmly to my heart
... then, we are one!!

Your Heart is so close to mine
... that the wonder of Your Heart ...
against my breast
... leaves me breathless ... full of the Holy Spirit
... sacredness throughout!

My hands, my body, my spirit
...all are lifted up to You, Lord!
You are my Bridegroom
... and I desire to be Your Bride
but I must be pure and chaste.

I pray that You find me acceptable
... and pleasing to You, Lord.
For my desire and love for You are
... so profound and entwined through
my total being
... which belongs to ... only You, Lord!

Human longing, human demise
If only I could ...
... hold you in my arms

... press Your Head against my chest
... feel the heat of Your Breath
    the moisture of Your Lips
    the softness of Your Hands
Longing, longing for these that do
not exist on earth
... but, only in Heaven.

Chapter VIII

"Arise to heaven with the Eucharist"

The Holy Eucharist

The Holy Spirit enkindled a Fire within me that has offered me many opportunities to grow spiritually closer to God and my fellow Christians. The most meaningful spiritual support and love I have received, has been through my attendance at Mass with the reception of the Holy Eucharist. It is from my closeness with the Lord that I would like to share with you my spiritual reflections of receiving the Holy Eucharist. I never realized how much I missed the Lord until I returned to Church and received Christ's Body and Blood in Communion, and now that I have received Him, I hunger for Him even more.

"And behold I am with you always."
(Matthew 28:20)

My Reflections on Receiving the Holy Eucharist

Pleasing is the feeling of the Holy Spirit within me,
    radiating glory to You, God.
Consuming, in receiving Your Eucharistic Banquet,
    fulfilling all needs and desires.

As I step up to the Lord's Altar and receive Him,
    I feel blessed.
The Eucharist to me,
    is the *closest* physical and spiritual way
    that I can *feel* God's Presence.

The Blessed Cup, the Chalice,
is His Blood - *Life Blood.*
    He tastes of such *sweetness* to my soul.
His Body, the Eucharist, within You, within me,
    how *close* can He get?

To be within us, spiritually and physically,
    united, together as one -
    we are together, one in Him.
There is no other food or drink!!

Christ is of us, within us, and we are one in Him.
We are one together, through Him in the Eucharist.

A *passionate love of union* with Him,
    nothing else can be looked upon -
    so deep, so profound, so fulfilling.
There is just nothing else, but Jesus.

A deep feeling of thirst, quenched by Your Blood.
A pit of hunger, fulfilled by Your Body
   total refreshment in You, Lord
   inspiring, uplifting my soul.

The Eucharist provides *so much* of Christ's Loving,
Caring, and Sharing, that I become filled up,
   fulfilled, and overflow with His Graces.
To reach out, and share with others,
   guiding them to Christ, the Eucharist.

When I receive the Body and Blood of
Christ in the Eucharist,
   the feeling of all-consuming,
   a craving for the Lord,
   is satisfied ... *a moment of peace.*
A total release of thoughts leads
into deep inspiration -
   nothing else can satisfy my waking moments.

The power and love experienced
when I receive the Holy Eucharist,
   is all more realized when I go just one day
   ... without it.

The manifestation of Christ's Body,
within one's own, and
the lifting of one's heart and soul by the Holy Spirit,
   is truly a *heightening experience,*
when ... *one allows God to take control.*

Opening oneself totally,
    giving oneself to the fulfilling, exciting,
    indescribable sensations when
    receiving Communion,
can never be surpassed by
anything else ... in this world.

God within us - ourselves within God.
All consuming, blinding us of all other desires,
    shielding from harm and evil –
    only good, only God happens, or exists ... here.

This is Heaven on earth.
This is Perfection.
This is God!!

Such is the sweet taste of the Eucharist,
Graces permeating one's body and soul
    uplifting and delighting.

So the desire for more continues
One cannot get enough of You ... Lord.

Your Body and Blood Lord,
the Eucharist and Precious Blood
such a vision to behold, and
such an honor to share, as a Eucharistic Minister.

It is so wonderful,
to be a part of the sharing of Christ's Body and Blood.

How wonderful it is to see You, Lord,
    in these people who receive You.
The peace is reflected on their faces, in their eyes,
    the happiness, the Lord is within them.

Oh God - this is Oneness with You,
    myself in You, You in myself,
    totally enmeshed in oneness!!

Lord,
You have broken and shared Your Body and Blood
with me and for me
so that I may be with You someday.
This is the only physical way
that I may experience and see
You while here on earth,
Your Heavenly Life Saving, Life Giving, Life
Promising Presence.

As I receive the Eucharist, I receive You,
You become a part of me,
and I with You, totally united, one.

Your Broken Body and Precious Blood blesses me,
enriches and uplifts my heart, mind, and soul to
indescribable heights,
and I relish each moment that you are with me.

My body is Your dwelling place, Your temple, and
Your vessel.
You fill me up with so much love,
that I long for more.

To share with others,
so that they too may experience this wonderful
love, hope and joy,
that You give in Your Supper, Your Banquet
Feast, the Holy Eucharist.

You give to me, Your True Love.

I breathe in Your Life - my soul
I breathe in Your Glory - my heart
I breathe in Your Warmth - my love
I breathe in Your Love - my essence of being.

A total consummation, is in receiving You
through ... prayers, inspiration,
and the Holy Eucharist.

Amen.

Breinigsville, PA USA
20 July 2010
242111BV00001B/2/P